Goal Getter

How to get the most out of
your past and get more
out of your future

Chris Robinson

First Printing, 2012

ISBN **978-0615747972**

Printed in the United States of America

Dedication

I would like to dedicate this book to my family who love and support me unconditionally. I would also like to specifically dedicate this book to our soon to be born 4th child who has yet to be named either Christopher David Robinson Jr. or David Christopher Robinson. Life is Grand, son! Live it to the fullest! Ada, Brex & Chase I love you dearly.

Goal Getter

How to get the most out of
your past and get more
out of your future

Table of Contents

Introduction

Are you looking for a process that allows you to set clear goals and achieve them? If so, you have chosen the right book. Welcome to what I call, "The Goal Getter Process" and let me explain why I wrote this method. It is because there are many goal setting methods out there but like so many others, I had to find something that worked for myself. This process came to me about two years ago and I've been utilizing it for the past two years with myself and also with clients. It has been just an incredible process to take people through!

Now, it is a lengthy process for most, but well worth it. In this day and age, everyone wants everything now and prefer the 'let's get this done' solution. So many people, when they sit down to write out there goals, if they even do, take 10 minutes and say to themselves – "Oh I've completed my goals for the year." But where people make mistakes is when they spend more time planning their vacation than they do planning their entire year. This process is not a 10-minute solution but, I assure you, once you are done with it you will be very pleased about your investment in yourself – just like I say in the subtitle, 'How to get the most of your past and get more out of future.'

You should pull everything you can out of the previous year before you move into the next year because if you go forward without even thinking about it, you're setting up the same hurdles you had last year. Have you ever asked yourself, "Why do I keep going around the same mountain?" The answer is because you are not pulling everything you can from the previous year.

Benefits of Goal Setting

Before we start the process, I want you to understand the benefits of setting goals because just as you will find in this section, the more benefits that are real to you, the more likely you are to take action and stick to it in tough times.

1. The first benefit is that it goal setting **directs our behavior** - whenever we set goals it directs our behavior. It gives us a target, it gives us a plan and it gives us a place to go to. If my goal is to get from the desk to the door in the room, then that is going to direct my behavior. I would not just aimlessly walk to the back wall of the office. I would not lie down on the floor. I would not to stay seated in the chair because my goal is to get to the door. When you set goals they direct your behavior.

2. When you set goals, **goals gives us a challenge** and I firmly believe if you're not being challenged, you are not growing and we want to always be in a state of growth and challenge ourselves to be better versions of ourselves. When we become complacent and don't have challenges, we start to drift and accept what life gives to us versus directing our lives. So when we set goals, it gives us something to strive for.

3. Goal setting **creates accountability**, first and foremost, with yourself. Many times when we set goals, we start to filter our goals and reason and rationalize with ourselves. We then begin to say things like, "Oh, maybe I can't do this," for whatever reason.

The reason most people don't want to write their goals down is because of the self-accountability that comes along with them. When you begin to write goals down you are questioning your current reality and for many that can be very difficult and struggle with the question of, "Do I really believe this to be true?"

When we write our goals down it is the start of accountability and if you want to take if further, get an accountability partner. Share your goals with other people and you will increase the accountability significantly

4. Goals **give you a basis of strategy**. Whenever you set goals, you have to have to have a plan in place, a strategy intact in order to meet that goal. You are not just going to haphazardly get to the door from your desk as we discussed earlier. When you set a new goal or goals you have to ask yourself, "How am I going to get to the door?"

Chances are you're not going to go *through* the desk, you know instead that you will go *around* the desk so you begin to walk. You know that once you get to the door, you're going to use the handle open the door if it is closed. By merely setting the goal it starts you on the path of setting a basis of strategy. You are going to provide a basis of strategy for whenever you set goals.

The 5 Areas For Setting Goals

There are five areas of reflection and goal setting and you want to reflect and set goals in these five different areas.

1. **Finances** - Finances are important because we all deal with it and if we look at the number one problem with relationships and marriages, it is money. I had the opportunity to hear a speaker at a conference being asked this question, "What is the number one tip you can give people?" He immediately responded, "Fix your money problem as soon as possible." He said to do this because it is not going to go away. Your life is going to be so much more different, not easier per say, but different when you fix that money problem.

2. **Health** - Your health is so important and a lot of people neglect it. You don't want to get to the point where you have to be overly concerned about your health and are backed into a corner before you say, "*Now* I have to change something about my health." Then you find yourself thinking I know I shouldn't eat all those bad meals and I should be exercising. I'm guilty of it, as well. I see myself as a fit person, not overweight, or in a bad health condition but inside… Am I shortening my life because I am not doing the right things with my health? So, while planning your goals, you want to take your health into account

3. **Business/Career** - So many people don't spend enough time planning their career. How are you going to get an promotion or advance your career? How can you become more educated? How can you learn more? How can you

progress more? How can you add more value to your organization? What does your progress look like inside of your career? What is your goal with your career? What have you learned from it this year? There are many questions that you can ask yourself about your career, and how to launch it to the next level.

I hear people brag all the time; "I have 15 years of experience in sales." It is often said that you have 1 year of experience 15 times. It's a shame to see that happen. Remember to reflect and set goals in your career.

4. **Relationships -** You want to make sure that you are setting goals, or looking at your relationships and asking, "How can I get this relationship to move forward?" Ask yourself what you did *right* in this relationship. What

you did wrong in this relationship and what can you do differently in this relationship?

I met a older gentleman sometime ago and what he said was this, "One of the most important things I've learned with being in business, and life in general, is first and foremost, putting your family on the calendar first before you do anything else because otherwise, your family gets your leftovers and that time goes by so fast that you'll regret it"

5. **Spiritual** - What did you get out of your spiritual life this year? What can you do to enhance it? This is a very important area and such an important key because we're mind, body and spirit and so you have to nurture the spiritual area of your life. If you are feeling burned out in other areas of your life, it may very well be because you are not nurturing the spiritual area of your life.

Reflecting

Looking at the five areas and taking time to reflect is critical in the goal setting process. When it comes to reflection there are five questions of contemplation to reflect in this process.

1. **The Small Victories** - When you are looking at those five areas, the first area to reflect on when you are looking at any particular area, is the small victories. So in your finances, what were some of the financial blessings you received? What were some of the victories? What were some of the victories in your health, spiritual life, etc? One of the keys of any progress is celebrating the small victories. It is the small victories that lead you to winning the big battles in your life. This allows us time to show gratitude for what did happen in our lives so we don't focus on what did not happen.

2. **The Miracles** - The miracles are the big things and those are the things you can say, "I don't know how this happened... It happened and I had nothing to do with it. It had to be God or it had to be someone else because I don't know how that happened." Reflect on each one of those areas because in each and every one of those five areas, I assure you, you had at least one miracle, if not several in your life.

3. **The Trials** - There is not a person on this planet that did not go through the previous year without some type of trial. What I know is that you are either going into a trial, you're in a trial or just coming out of a trial so we want to take a look back at those trials and say, "How did you overcome that trial? How did you respond in that trial? What could we have done to prevent those trials?" Again, going back through each one of those five areas, asking what were the trials? Look at the trials so that you are prepared for the

following year so you don't have to deal with them the same way if it was in fact handled the wrong way.

4. **The Lessons You Learned** - This is my favorite part of reflection by far. This is serious and I love this, my pastor said this and it blew my mind, "If you can't tell me what you learned this year, you have to repeat it next year."

Take the time here to write out the full lessons. Not just the one word. What were some actual lessons that you learned? For me, I can share several of the lessons that I learned in the previous year. The number one lesson was that people do get what they want, including me. Number two was that there is always a cheaper, faster, easier way to do things. Those are just two of the lessons and I have many, many lessons that I learned so ask yourself, "What did I learn?" and expand on the full lesson.

5. **Examine Your Calendar** - In this part of reflection go back through your calendar for the full year to examine day-by-day three key things: People, Places and Productivity.

People - When you go back through your calendar, find people that you should spend time with, people you shouldn't have spent time with and people with whom not much happened at all.

Places - What events, what outings or what conferences did you attend that you would say would be beneficial to attend again this year or to not attend this year?

Productivity – Here's where you look at the results, "What areas were you most productive in? What were the most productive activities? What were the most productive courses you attended? What were the most productive seminars? Who were the most productive people you were around?"

When going through the calendar, work through your calendar, day-by-day through the entire year and go through all the people and places that where you spent time throughout the entire year and highlight them – red, yellow or green.

Red people and places are people that nothing positive happened with this person or place at all and actually a lot of bad things may have happened in some cases.

Yellow people and places are those that had nothing good or nothing bad that happened. You don't have to avoid them but don't pursue them either.

Green people and places are for good places and good relationships that you need to invest in to build them up to a higher level.

By going through the reflection section of this process it really allows for you to turn good experiences into valuable experiences while allowing yourself to get the most out of the past before moving on to establish new goals.

Ten Keys To Setting Goals

1. **Write Down The Goals** - You hear it time and time again. What's holding you back? If you have never done it, do it! Writing your goals down even goes back to the Bible.

    Habakkuk 2:2 says, "Write down the revelation and make it plain on tablets so that a runner may run with it."

    Something magical happens, something special happens, when you go from your mind, to writing it down on a piece of paper. There is something that transfers and I'm not able to explain it but I know works!

2. **Write Down The Known Action Steps** - This is critical because from here to any goal that you want to reach you have to realize that there are goals with an 'S'. You don't have to know every single step in order to get there.

The way I teach it is that if you want to get from where you are now to somewhere else and it is dark outside, then you have to have your headlights on. Your headlights don't show you the entire way, but what it does show is about 150 feet ahead of you and that is all you need to be able to see how to make it from where you are now to where you want to be.

Continue to travel those 150 feet in front of you and the rest will reveal itself along the way. Sometimes you will be able to see further but take ground where you can. Take the action steps that you know of **NOW.**

3. **List Your Current Position** - Where are you now financially? Where are you currently with your health? Where are you in your spiritual life?

When you list your current position this brings realism to the optimism of setting your goals by listing your current position. Now don't get discouraged or hang out here if you are nowhere near where you want to be, just be sure to know where you are.

Let's say for example you make $25,000, don't say, "I want to make $1 million," because come the second week of January, like the masses of the world, you'll clear your goals because it just seems too far out of reach. Now don't get me wrong, I am not saying it is impossible to go from $25,000 to $1 million in a single year but let's be real - the odds are slim! You want to set attainable goals that push you. Every time you reach a goal it reinforces that you *can* do it!

4. **List The Benefits** - The benefits are the *why* you want to achieve the goal. This is so important because the more benefits of why you want to achieve the goal that you can come up with, the more likely you are continue reaching for that goal when times get difficult. So you want to list out as many benefits as you possibly can because that is going to reinforce the motivation that is going to get you to where you want to be.

5. **Identify The Obstacles Risk** - There is going to be opposition between you and any goal that you want to go after. Often times we don't think about the obstacles and we just think, "I'll get there," but guess what happens? Life. So we want to make sure that we can think of as many obstacles as we can, again this is not an area

that we want to spend too much time in and dwell on, but we want to think of what will be some of the obstacles that we'll come across. What will be some of the risks that we will come across? Are there things I'm going to have to give up? Are there things that I'm going to have to change? Making sure that we identify those things before we get started.

6. **Ask Yourself; Am I Going To Need To Acquire New Knowledge?** Many people want to go from one level to the next but they are unaware that they need to know something new. What you have here, won't get you there, is often said. So you want to make sure that if you say you want to achieve this goal, what is it that you need to learn? What is it that you don't know that you need to know? As I stated earlier you don't need to have the entire way laid out in steps but what I do know, is that at times,

new levels require new knowledge to be learned.

7. **Identify The Investment That Is Required To Obtain The Goal** - When it comes to your goal, you are going to have to make an investment in two areas. The first one being time and then often the second investment is going to be money. So you want to add up the total cost.

I know a friend that was thinking of getting into a coaching program and this person was struggling to get by and they thought, "If I just get into this program, it will change everything," and yes, I completely agreed, but I knew this individual was only looking at the entry not the total investment. I asked them to look at a few things that maybe they were not considering, such as the cost of idea implementation of ideas, the cost of going to the events, travel costs, etc. A lot of the times, we don't know the whole cost. So we have to identify the investment that is going to be required to obtain the goal.

8. **Get A Support Team** – Previously, we talked about goals and how goals create accountability for you, but if you really want to enhance that, then get a support team of positive people.

You can't have just any type of growth orientated support people. You need forward thinking and progressive people around you that are going to build you up and not tear you down. You don't want to get a support team that is going to agree with your cop-out. You don't want to get a support team that is going to agree with your excuses. You want to get a support team that will help you strive towards your goals.

9. **Set Deadlines On Small And Large Goals** - The reason that we want to set a deadline is because we want to create a sense of urgency. What we don't watch and what we don't gauge doesn't get done. This provides a level of measurement and when we look at goals, there are many small goals on the way to the big goal. So we want to set timelines and parameters, to ensure that we meet those milestones on the way to those large goals.

10. **Reward And Celebrate Along The Way** - Goals can be tough to reach and many people get overwhelmed and discouraged because they look at that end goal and can't see the progress they have made. You may not be where they want to be and what we have to tell ourselves is that we are not where we used to be and reward and celebrate along the way.

If, and this is a big IF…if you take the time to invest in yourself and go step by step through the action guide following this chapter, unlike 97% of the people who read this book, I can assure you that you are going to get more out of your past and even more out of your future.

You have come this far; only *you* can limit your potential take the next step and fill out the guide. It's your future… Do It NOW!

Action Guide

The Goal Getter process has been laid out for you step by step in the following pages for every area of setting goals. If you have any questions contact me at chris@r3-coaching.com

Finances

In the previous year what were the small victories in your finances?

1. _____

2. _____

3. _____

4. _____

5. _____

6. _____

7. _____

8. _____

9. _____

10. _____

In the previous year what were miracles occurred in your finances?

1. _____

2. _____

3. _____

4. _____

5. _____

6. _____

7. _____

8. _____

9. _____

10. _____

What were the lessons you learned about finances this past year?

1. _____

2. _____

3. _____

4. _____

5. _____

6. _____

7. _____

8. _____

9. _____

10. _____

What are the top 3 goals you want to accomplish with your finances?

1. _____

2. _____

3. _____

Major Goal #1

1. What is the 1st major goal you want to achieve with your finances?

    _____

2. What action steps do you know now?

    _____

    _____

3. Where are you currently in regards to this goal?

    _____

4. What are the benefits of achieving this goal?

    _____

    _____

    _____

5. What are some potential obstacles that could prevent you from reaching this goal?

    _____

    _____

    _____

6. Is there going to be new knowledge required? If so what can you do to begin to learn?

_____

_____

7. What investment will be required to obtain this goal?

_____

_____

8. Who can be a part of your support team?

_____

_____

9. What is the date that you will reach this goal?

_____

10. How & when will you reward yourself along the way?

_____

_____

_____

Major Goal #2

1. What is the 2nd major goal you want to achieve with your finances?

   _____

2. What action steps do you know now?

   _____

   _____

3. Where are you currently in regards to this goal?

   _____

4. What are the benefits of achieving this goal?

   _____

   _____

   _____

5. What are some potential obstacles that could prevent you from reaching this goal?

   _____

   _____

   _____

6. Is there going to be new knowledge required? If so what can you do to begin to learn?

_____

_____

7. What investment will be required to obtain this goal?

_____

_____

8. Who can be a part of your support team?

_____

_____

9. What is the date that you will reach this goal?

_____

10. How & when will you reward yourself along the way?

_____

_____

Major Goal #3

1. What is the 3rd major goal you want to achieve with your finances?

   _____

2. What action steps do you know now?

   _____

   _____

3. Where are you currently in regards to this goal?

   _____

4. What are the benefits of achieving this goal?

   _____

   _____

   _____

5. What are some potential obstacles that could prevent you from reaching this goal?

   _____

   _____

   _____

6. Is there going to be new knowledge required? If so what can you do to begin to learn?

_____

_____

7. What investment will be required to obtain this goal?

_____

_____

8. Who can be a part of your support team?

_____

_____

9. What is the date that you will reach this goal?

_____

10. How & when will you reward yourself along the way?

_____

_____

Health

In the previous year what were the small victories in your Health?

1. _____

2. _____

3. _____

4. _____

5. _____

6. _____

7. _____

8. _____

9. _____

10. _____

In the previous year what were miracles occurred in your Health?

1. _____

2. _____

3. _____

4. _____

5. _____

6. _____

7. _____

8. _____

9. _____

10. _____

What were the lessons you learned about your health this past year?

1. _____

2. _____

3. _____

4. _____

5. _____

6. _____

7. _____

8. _____

9. _____

10. _____

What are the top 3 goals you want to accomplish with your Health?

1. _____

2. _____

3. _____

Major Goal #1

1. What is the 1st major goal you want to achieve with your finances?

   _____

2. What action steps do you know now?

   _____

   _____

3. Where are you currently in regards to this goal?

   _____

4. What are the benefits of achieving this goal?

   _____

   _____

   _____

5. What are some potential obstacles that could prevent you from reaching this goal?

   _____

   _____

   _____

6. Is there going to be new knowledge required? If so what can you do to begin to learn?

_____

_____

7. What investment will be required to obtain this goal?

_____

_____

8. Who can be a part of your support team?

_____

_____

9. What is the date that you will reach this goal?

_____

10. How & when will you reward yourself along the way?

_____

_____

_____

Major Goal #2

1. What is the 2nd major goal you want to achieve with your Health?

   _____

2. What action steps do you know now?

   _____

   _____

3. Where are you currently in regards to this goal?

   _____

4. What are the benefits of achieving this goal?

   _____

   _____

   _____

5. What are some potential obstacles that could prevent you from reaching this goal?

   _____

   _____

   _____

6. Is there going to be new knowledge required? If so what can you do to begin to learn?

_____

_____

7. What investment will be required to obtain this goal?

_____

_____

8. Who can be a part of your support team?

_____

_____

9. What is the date that you will reach this goal?

_____

10. How & when will you reward yourself along the way?

_____

_____

_____

Major Goal #3

1. What is the 3rd major goal you want to achieve with your Health?

   _____

2. What action steps do you know now?

   _____

   _____

3. Where are you currently in regards to this goal?

   _____

4. What are the benefits of achieving this goal?

   _____

   _____

   _____

5. What are some potential obstacles that could prevent you from reaching this goal?

   _____

   _____

   _____

6. Is there going to be new knowledge required? If so what can you do to begin to learn?

_____

_____

7. What investment will be required to obtain this goal?

_____

_____

8. Who can be a part of your support team?

_____

_____

9. What is the date that you will reach this goal?

_____

10. How & when will you reward yourself along the way?

_____

_____

_____

Business/Career

In the previous year what were the small victories in your business/career?

1. _____

2. _____

3. _____

4. _____

5. _____

6. _____

7. _____

8. _____

9. _____

10. _____

In the previous year what were miracles occurred in your business/career?

1. _____

2. _____

3. _____

4. _____

5. _____

6. _____

7. _____

8. _____

9. _____

10. _____

What were the lessons you learned about your business/career this past year?

1. _____

2. _____

3. _____

4. _____

5. _____

6. _____

7. _____

8. _____

9. _____

10. _____

What are the top 3 goals you want to accomplish with your Business/Career?

1. _____

2. _____

3. _____

Major Goal #1

1. What is the 1st major goal you want to achieve with your Business/Career?

   _____

2. What action steps do you know now?

   _____

   _____

3. Where are you currently in regards to this goal?

   _____

4. What are the benefits of achieving this goal?

   _____

   _____

   _____

5. What are some potential obstacles that could prevent you from reaching this goal?

   _____

   _____

   _____

6. Is there going to be new knowledge required? If so what can you do to begin to learn?

_____

_____

7. What investment will be required to obtain this goal?

_____

_____

8. Who can be a part of your support team?

_____

_____

9. What is the date that you will reach this goal?

_____

10. How & when will you reward yourself along the way?

_____

_____

_____

Major Goal #2

1. What is the 2nd major goal you want to achieve with your Business/Career?

    _____

2. What action steps do you know now?

    _____

    _____

3. Where are you currently in regards to this goal?

    _____

4. What are the benefits of achieving this goal?

    _____

    _____

    _____

5. What are some potential obstacles that could prevent you from reaching this goal?

    _____

    _____

    _____

6. Is there going to be new knowledge required? If so what can you do to begin to learn?

_____

_____

7. What investment will be required to obtain this goal?

_____

_____

8. Who can be a part of your support team?

_____

_____

9. What is the date that you will reach this goal?

_____

10. How & when will you reward yourself along the way?

_____

_____

_____

Major Goal #3

1. What is the 3rd major goal you want to achieve with your Business/Career?

   _____

2. What action steps do you know now?

   _____

   _____

3. Where are you currently in regards to this goal?

   _____

4. What are the benefits of achieving this goal?

   _____

   _____

   _____

5. What are some potential obstacles that could prevent you from reaching this goal?

   _____

   _____

   _____

6. Is there going to be new knowledge required? If so what can you do to begin to learn?

_____

_____

7. What investment will be required to obtain this goal?

_____

_____

8. Who can be a part of your support team?

_____

_____

9. What is the date that you will reach this goal?

_____

10. How & when will you reward yourself along the way?

_____

_____

_____

Relationships

In the previous year what were the small victories in your Relationships?

1. _____

2. _____

3. _____

4. _____

5. _____

6. _____

7. _____

8. _____

9. _____

10. _____

In the previous year what were miracles occurred in your Relationships?

1. _____

2. _____

3. _____

4. _____

5. _____

6. _____

7. _____

8. _____

9. _____

10. _____

What were the lessons you learned about
Relationships this past year?

1. _____

2. _____

3. _____

4. _____

5. _____

6. _____

7. _____

8. _____

9. _____

10. _____

What are the top 3 goals you want to accomplish with your Relationships?

1. _____

2. _____

3. _____

Major Goal #1

1. What is the 1st major goal you want to achieve with your Relationships?

   _____

2. What action steps do you know now?

   _____

   _____

3. Where are you currently in regards to this goal?

   _____

4. What are the benefits of achieving this goal?

   _____

   _____

   _____

5. What are some potential obstacles that could prevent you from reaching this goal?

   _____

   _____

   _____

6. Is there going to be new knowledge required? If so what can you do to begin to learn?

_____

_____

7. What investment will be required to obtain this goal?

_____

_____

8. Who can be a part of your support team?

_____

_____

9. What is the date that you will reach this goal?

_____

10. How & when will you reward yourself along the way?

_____

_____

_____

Major Goal #2

1. What is the 2nd major goal you want to achieve with your Relationships?

   _____

2. What action steps do you know now?

   _____

   _____

3. Where are you currently in regards to this goal?

   _____

4. What are the benefits of achieving this goal?

   _____

   _____

   _____

5. What are some potential obstacles that could prevent you from reaching this goal?

   _____

81

6. Is there going to be new knowledge required? If so what can you do to begin to learn?

_____

_____

7. What investment will be required to obtain this goal?

_____

_____

8. Who can be a part of your support team?

_____

_____

9. What is the date that you will reach this goal?

_____

10. How & when will you reward yourself along the way?

_____

_____

_____

Major Goal #3

1. What is the 3rd major goal you want to achieve with your Relationships?

   _____

2. What action steps do you know now?

   _____

   _____

3. Where are you currently in regards to this goal?

   _____

4. What are the benefits of achieving this goal?

   _____

   _____

   _____

5. What are some potential obstacles that could prevent you from reaching this goal?

   _____

   _____

   _____

6. Is there going to be new knowledge required? If so what can you do to begin to learn?

    _____

    _____

7. What investment will be required to obtain this goal?

    _____

    _____

8. Who can be a part of your support team?

    _____

    _____

9. What is the date that you will reach this goal?

    _____

10. How & when will you reward yourself along the way?

    _____

    _____

    _____

Spiritual

In the previous year what were the small victories in your Spiritual life?

1. _____

2. _____

3. _____

4. _____

5. _____

6. _____

7. _____

8. _____

9. _____

10. _____

In the previous year what were miracles occurred in your Spiritual life?

1. _____

2. _____

3. _____

4. _____

5. _____

6. _____

7. _____

8. _____

9. _____

10. _____

What were the lessons you learned about your spiritual life this past year?

1. _____

2. _____

3. _____

4. _____

5. _____

6. _____

7. _____

8. _____

9. _____

10. _____

What are the top 3 goals you want to accomplish with your Relationships?

1. _____

2. _____

3. _____

Major Goal #1

1. What is the 1st major goal you want to achieve with your Spiritual Life?

   _____

2. What action steps do you know now?

   _____

   _____

3. Where are you currently in regards to this goal?

   _____

4. What are the benefits of achieving this goal?

   _____

   _____

   _____

5. What are some potential obstacles that could prevent you from reaching this goal?

   _____

   _____

   _____

6. Is there going to be new knowledge required? If so what can you do to begin to learn?

_____

_____

7. What investment will be required to obtain this goal?

_____

_____

8. Who can be a part of your support team?

_____

_____

9. What is the date that you will reach this goal?

_____

10. How & when will you reward yourself along the way?

_____

_____

_____

Major Goal #2

1. What is the 2nd major goal you want to achieve with your Spiritual Life?

   _____

2. What action steps do you know now?

   _____

   _____

3. Where are you currently in regards to this goal?

   _____

4. What are the benefits of achieving this goal?

   _____

   _____

   _____

5. What are some potential obstacles that could prevent you from reaching this goal?

   _____

   _____

   _____

6. Is there going to be new knowledge required? If so what can you do to begin to learn?

_____

_____

7. What investment will be required to obtain this goal?

_____

_____

8. Who can be a part of your support team?

_____

_____

9. What is the date that you will reach this goal?

_____

10. How & when will you reward yourself along the way?

_____

_____

_____

Major Goal #3

1. What is the 3rd major goal you want to achieve with your Spiritual Life?

   _____

2. What action steps do you know now?

   _____

   _____

3. Where are you currently in regards to this goal?

   _____

4. What are the benefits of achieving this goal?

   _____

   _____

   _____

5. What are some potential obstacles that could prevent you from reaching this goal?

   _____

   _____

   _____

6. Is there going to be new knowledge required? If so what can you do to begin to learn?

_____

_____

7. What investment will be required to obtain this goal?

_____

_____

8. Who can be a part of your support team?

_____

_____

9. What is the date that you will reach this goal?

_____

10. How & when will you reward yourself along the way?

_____

_____

_____

People, Places & Productivity

Calendar Review

People

Green (need to invest in relationship)

1. _____

2. _____

3. _____

4. _____

5. _____

6. _____

7. _____

8. _____

9. _____

10. _____

Yellow (don't avoid but don't pursue)

1. _____

2. _____

3. _____

4. _____

5. _____

6. _____

7. _____

8. _____

9. _____

10. _____

Red (do not pursue)

1. _____

2. _____

3. _____

4. _____

5. _____

6. _____

7. _____

8. _____

9. _____

10. _____

Places

Green (need to invest in relationship)

1. _____

2. _____

3. _____

4. _____

5. _____

6. _____

7. _____

8. _____

9. _____

10. _____

Yellow (don't avoid but don't pursue)

1. _____

2. _____

3. _____

4. _____

5. _____

6. _____

7. _____

8. _____

9. _____

10. _____

Red (do not pursue)

1. _____

2. _____

3. _____

4. _____

5. _____

6. _____

7. _____

8. _____

9. _____

10. _____

Productivity

Areas you were most productive

Green (need to invest in relationship)

1. _____

2. _____

3. _____

4. _____

5. _____

6. _____

7. _____

8. _____

9. _____

10. _____

Yellow (don't avoid but don't pursue)

1. _____

2. _____

3. _____

4. _____

5. _____

6. _____

7. _____

8. _____

9. _____

10. _____

Red (do not pursue)

1. _____

2. _____

3. _____

4. _____

5. _____

6. _____

7. _____

8. _____

9. _____

10. _____

About the Author

Chris Robinson is the founder of R3 Coaching, a company dedicated to helping individuals and businesses achieve their personal and business growth goals. Chris's speaking; group training and one-on-one coaching has helped many businesses.

Chris found his leadership beginnings as a sales representative that quickly advanced 3 positions in 5 years to a Senior Sales Manager for the largest vehicle service contract company in the United States. Chris quickly realized his niche and passion for recognizing the strengths and overcoming the weak areas of business early on. Chris helped grow the company from 18 employees to over 700. After experiencing this tremendous growth and recognizing his desire and ability to encourage, inspire, and communicate life-altering success principles to others, R3 Coaching was born.

Chris has the ability to assess a situation, recognize the problem, and lay a solid, workable plan of action that empowers the business or individual involved. Whether it is a team of 200 telemarketers, a new business without clear direction or an individual looking to climb the corporate ladder, Chris will get you where you want to go. Chris's training will enrich your attitude, rekindle your determination to succeed, and expand your self-confidence. You'll come away empowered, centered, and focused on your determined goals.

How would YOU like to Achieve Extraordinary Success for Your Team, Your Company, & Yourself?

As an independent certified speaker, coach and trainer for The John Maxwell Team, Chris can bring your team to new level of success with these 5 outstanding Programs!

> ➤ Becoming a person of Influence
> ➤ Leadership Gold
> ➤ Everyone communicates few connect
>
> ➤ Put your dream to the test
> ➤ How to be a real success

To schedule Chris to Speak at Your Next Conference, Meeting or Company Training Call Today! 636-336-2830

www.liftmylid.com
www.r3-coaching.com